AF615398

Any Christian Can

Any Christian Can

A Personal Guide to Individual Ministry

Douglas A. Elliott

A Key-Word Book
WORD BOOKS, Publisher
Waco, Texas

ISBN 0-8499-4125-3
Library of Congress catalog card number: 79-66522
Printed in the United States of America

Dedicated to Eddie, Margie, Bill, and Sue who are my inner circle of chapter 9.

And, to Jean. She knew it should be written—and she believed that I could do it.

Contents

1. Ministries Available
Ordinary People Please Apply

"If only I had special musical talent—then I could really minister to other people."

"If only I could preach and teach—then I would be used to affect the lives of others."

"If only I could be at the right place when all the correct circumstances would catapult me into some spectacular ministry—then I could . . ."

"If only . . . then I could . . ."

"If only . . . then I would . . ."

"If only . . ."

Sound familiar?

You have dreamed of someday being endowed with a special gift so that you could do spectacular things in ministry to other people.

But that special gift or opportunity never seems to come, does it? And you sink into a slough of depression, feeling guilty and left out because of your ordinariness.

Well, join the crowd.

God must place special value on ordinary people because he made so many of us. If we waste our time feeling sorry that we are not more spectacular we may miss the vital, everyday ministries that God gives to each of us.

Many of us feel a lack of self-worth because, though we may be gifted at certain things, those things are not encouraged or considered important. If someone tells us, "You make a wonderful apple pie," we are likely to say, "Thank you, but it really doesn't matter. I'm not a famous singer, clergyman, teacher or businessman that anyone has ever heard of." Rarely are we told that making a good apple pie is important in itself. We need to learn that everything that we do well is worthwhile and can be used in ministry to others.

Christians often talk of "serving the Lord" as if it were some spiritual activity that they hope to perform someday. I have heard countless people say, "I wish that I didn't have to work at my ordinary job. Then I could serve the Lord full time. Maybe I'll be able to retire early so that I can devote the rest of my life to ministering."

Each day, whatever our jobs, we have ministry opportunities. Scripturally, "serving the Lord" is the faithful, day-by-day exercise of the ordinary gifts that God has given to each of us. Not someday, in a nebulous future, but now—today.

Looking back, I can see that the practical shaping of my life was done, for the most part, by people who did not have outstanding talents or abilities.

I have been helped by a seventy-five-year-old church

custodian who took the time to listen to me when, as an eight-year-old boy, I arrived early for Sunday school.

I have been moved by the words of "Jesus, Jesus, Jesus," sung by a crippled, retarded child.

My spirits have been lifted by a deaf and mute Korean orphan girl "singing" the Lord's Prayer in sign language.

I have been encouraged in my faith by an elderly lady who could do nothing more than smile from her hospital bed.

I have been prodded to pick up the pieces of my life by a friend who took the risk to stand beside me when everything seemed to be crumbling.

None of these people was spectacular—but they ministered to me in a way that I needed at the time.

I don't remember who spoke at my college graduation, nor do I recall much of what he said. But his opening illustration has stayed with me.

It seems that the thousand residents of a small valley village received their water supply from cool springs high in the surrounding mountains. For more than a decade they paid a retired man $500 each year to make a weekly climb to clean leaves and twigs from the springs so that the water would continue to flow clean and uninterrupted.

He did his job faithfully and unnoticed year after year. The village residents took their water supply for granted.

Eventually the aging man could no longer negotiate the long journey safely. He told village officials that they would have to find someone to replace him.

Since the water had flowed freely for many years,

and since budget money was tight, they decided to retire the old man without replacing him.

A month went by, and the people noticed a reduction in water pressure. They attributed this condition to an unusually dry summer.

Another two weeks passed. One morning they woke up to find a mere trickle of water coming from their faucets. Town workers began to trace the pipes, assuming that there had been a break in the line.

Their search led them to the source of the problem. The springs were plugged with leaves and other debris. At last they realized the value of the service which the old man had performed for so many years.

He was an ordinary man, doing an important, ordinary job. The "Keeper of the Springs" had made a valuable contribution to the daily welfare and comfort of his fellow villagers.

For centuries, the Colorado River, in its wild fourteen-hundred-mile descent from the Rocky Mountains to the Pacific Ocean, destroyed crops, lives, and property as the melting snows in spring and summer flooded low-lying farm land along the route. In late summer and fall the river dried to a trickle and crops and livestock withered and died. Its uncontrolled flow provided either too much or too little.

Today, Hoover Dam ponderously straddles the line between Nevada and Arizona. With its three and one-quarter million cubic yards of concrete, standing seven hundred and twenty-six feet high, it controls billions of gallons of water in its reservoir, Lake Mead. It now provides regulated, year-round irrigation to three quarters of a million acres of land in this country and nearly one quarter of a million in Mexico.

One has only to visit the dam to imagine the tremendous determination required to overcome the engineering obstacles which the project presented.

The dam was built over a period of seven years through the efforts of hundreds of ordinary people who faithfully performed their duties each day by applying their varied, individual skills.

In a similar way, the construction of the Body of Christ continues today—largely through the ministries of people like you, who faithfully do what they can do best.

This book is written to help you in your ordinary, practical ministering to other people.

You *can* do it.

2. Thieves, Prostitutes, Drunks, and the Holy Spirit

Cultivating Attitudes for Ministering

Yes, you *can* do it. But, in order to begin, there are four fundamental questions which need to be explored honestly.

1. *Are you able to put people first?*

We moved into our "new" one-hundred-year-old house on Memorial Day weekend. It is located on the main street of a small country town sixty miles north of New York City.

Since its previous owners were long-time community residents, we became known as "the people who bought the Gallagher house."

In spite of its age, the house was in remarkably good repair, except for need of redecorating. Because of the potential which we saw in the old place we eagerly set about painting and wallpapering the whole house, room by room.

Time available for such work was limited. So, every spare minute was crammed with major and minor projects.

We soon discovered a conflict developing inside us. Neighbors and new friends enjoyed stopping by to chat about the touches that we were adding to the house. All of these people-to-people contacts took time away from scheduled chores.

One Saturday four different families dropped in, each for half an hour or longer. This put me two hours behind schedule for that day!

How should we react to such "interruptions"? We took our cue from Jesus' response to an expert in Moses' law who asked, "Who is my neighbor?"

Jesus answered with a story about an unfortunate traveler who was attacked by bandits. They stole his clothes and money. Then they beat him up and left him near death beside the road.

A Hebrew priest passed by, saw the helpless victim lying there, and deliberately crossed to the other side of the road and continued his journey. A second Hebrew, one who knew the minute interpretations of religious law, actually walked over to look at the dying man. But then, he too, went on his way.

Finally, along came a person whose ancestry made him an object of Jewish scorn. Being part Jew and part pagan, he was considered lower than a Gentile. This Samaritan, however, responded to human need with compassion. He stopped his own trip and bandaged the victim's wounds. Then he took the injured man to an inn and stayed with him throughout the night.

The next day, before leaving, the Samaritan gave the innkeeper some money to care for the needs of the wounded traveler. He even promised to pay whatever additional bills might accumulate.

Jesus indicated that the compassionate traveler loved his neighbor as himself and so fulfilled one of the two principles of God's law: love God, and love your neighbor. He was "people-centered."

We agreed that, regardless of limited time, regardless of the amount of work to be done on the old house, "people relationships" must always take top priority in our lives.

It isn't always easy. But now, when people stop for a visit, the work ceases and we enjoy their company. These developing relationships are among the most rewarding that we have ever had. And, sometimes, they are opportunities to minister in Christ's name.

I know a lady who insisted that her children attend Sunday school each week so that they would receive perfect attendance certificates. Regular Sunday school participation is desirable, but, in this case, the rigid schedule kept the children from an occasional weekend visit to the grandparents' home—an opportunity that would have been beneficial to all concerned.

The temptation to put personal schedules and group programs before person-to-person encounters can subtly rob us of rewarding ministry opportunities.

Part of learning to put people first is viewing them as individuals—even when they are part of a group.

We are conditioned to judge the success of an event by attendance figures—the higher the number, the greater the success. This formula may be valid when evaluating some form of spectator entertainment. But it is not legitimate to assess the success or failure of a study class or worship service, where the deepest needs of people are involved, by the number in attendance. Under these circumstances, a crowd of five hundred is not only a group; it is made up of five hundred unique individuals who happen to be in the same place at the same time.

Several dozen preachers were asked, "In what aspect of your work do you sense the most accomplishment and success?" The surveyors expected the clergymen to say, "Preaching," or, "Teaching."

But most of the pastors responded that helping people on a one-to-one basis gave them the strongest feeling that they were fulfilling their ministries.

As one man put it, "When I get my knees under someone else's kitchen table and talk about life as it really is—that's where the rubber meets the road."

What will it be then?

People or paint?

People or programs?

People or schedules?

Our answers to these questions will determine the possibility of our person-to-person outreach.

2. *Do you really care?*

Caring is a rare commodity in our day. People don't seem to take the time to express concern for others. When we do show that we care, we are different, and people pay attention.

Early in my Christian experience I believed that I had to be "different" if nonbelievers were to be attracted to Christ through me. So, I concentrated on creating a "different" behavior pattern. In capsule, my approach was, "I am a Christian. I am different. I don't smoke, drink, play cards or go to the movies. See how wonderful it is to be a Christian? Why don't you become one?" I was underwhelmed by the responses.

Then I began to ask, "What attracted people to Jesus? Was it his behavior pattern? Was it the things that he didn't do?" No. The strongest attractions were his care and concern for individuals.

His conversation with a Samaritan woman at the town well is but one illustration that Jesus' compassion always reached through unacceptable, even sinful, behavior to the person.

She was a community outcast because of her illicit relationships. Jesus knew all about her. He said. "You have had five husbands, and you aren't married to the man that you're living with now."

He also knew that associating with her would subject him to the "birds of a feather flock together" accusation. And besides, Jews just weren't supposed to converse with Samaritans. His own disciples were surprised to find him talking to this woman alone.

But that didn't matter to Jesus. His concern was for her need. And, as a result, she came to recognize him as the Messiah.

Jesus soundly denounced religious leaders whose minute, repressive laws rode rough-shod over people.

It was his caring association with thieves, drunks, and prostitutes that ran him afoul of their legalistic system and eventually contributed to his crucifixion.

The badge of Christianity is not some well-defined behavior pattern. It is compassion. Much "accepted Christian behavior" varies geographically and is the result of man-made tradition. The need for concerned caring is universal.

Some people would shun Anita because of her occupation. She works from 9:00 P.M. until 5:00 A.M. as a cocktail waitress. Several years ago she decided to care for her eighty-three-year-old invalid mother at home instead of putting her in a nursing hospital. The income and hours of her job make this possible. Though Anita does not claim to be "religious," her kind of caring is admirable.

Could you offer care and understanding to a cocktail waitress? Or, would her occupation keep you from showing compassion? Would you be able to see through her job to Anita, the person?

3. *Are you flexible?*

The Las Vegas Strip, lined with its plush hotels and opulent gambling casinos, seems like a strange setting for Christian ministering. But Jim Reid, Chaplain of the Strip, is carrying out an effective outreach almost single-handedly as he moves with ease in the world of gamblers, casino workers, entertainers, musicians, and stagehands. Each day he confronts the devastating effects of loneliness, alienation, prostitution, drug addiction, and materialism.

Jim is able to affect the lives of needy people because he has freed himself to use unconventional methods, as evidenced by his regular, casino-based worship services. I suppose that some would even consider a few of his methods "unacceptable," but this flexibility of method is a key to the success of Jim's ministry. He is reaching people who probably would not respond to standard programs of outreach.

If you wish to minister in an effective way, you too will have to free yourself to use a variety of ministering methods. Recognize that it takes "different strokes for different folks." The Gospel message remains constant. The methods of communication must change to meet a large spectrum of human needs.

Jesus was flexible in his methods of helping people. He taught large crowds, but he also engaged in private conversations. He illustrated his truths with a variety of miracles, all performed in different ways. Some people were healed with a word, others with a touch. Others were anointed with mud. A few were cured without even seeing Jesus.

Our opportunities for personal outreach will increase as we develop the facility to move easily from one method to another in meeting people's needs.

4. *Can you be patient with the Holy Spirit?*

The art of bricklaying requires patient endurance. The tradesman sets one brick at a time, and eventually the job is finished.

The spiritual bricklaying that is accomplished in people's lives also requires patient endurance. It is done, line upon line, precept upon precept.

Saul's conversion (Acts 9) is often presented as a pattern for all conversions—instantaneous and spectacular. Actually, it is a rare exception. Most conversions take time and patience—the bricks are added one at a time.

We tend to overlook the fact that shortly after he was converted, Paul spent three years in seclusion getting his spiritual bearings. This is in sharp contrast to the "celebrity Christianity" trend which we see today. Often a well-known athlete, entertainer, or political figure is converted and instantly projected into important public ministry and responsibility. Sometimes the results are damaging, especially to the newly converted individual who has not had time to build a strong base for his new faith.

Undoubtedly there were many ordinary people behind the scenes who contributed to the step-by-step building process in Paul's new life.

Spiritual birth and growth take time. As you plant the seeds of ministry in other people's lives, recognize that you may not be the one to nurture and harvest the spiritual crop. Free yourself from the pride and frustration of always wanting to see astounding results immediately.

The Holy Spirit is the One who sovereignly makes the seeds grow at his predetermined pace. He is not bound to operate on a human time schedule. One day with the Lord is as a thousand years and a thousand years as one day.

Over the years I have seen ordinary people develop fruitful personal ministries because of their people-centered compassion, their flexibility, and their patience.

As we grow in our capacity to care, to select the appropriate methods, and to rely patiently on God's Spirit, our opportunities to minister to others will increase.

3. God with Skin On

Ministering through, to the Person

One sticky, summer evening, shortly after eight-year-old Suzanne went to bed, a severe storm broke loose. The first hard clap of thunder sent the child running down the steps.

"Mom, I'm scared," she said.

After a few moments of quiet comfort, the mother said, "Now, there is nothing to be afraid of. You go back upstairs and go to sleep."

The youngster responded with an uncertain "Okay," and returned to her room.

Several minutes passed, then a crackling strike of lightning drove her downstairs again.

"I'm still scared," she whimpered.

This time her mother, with a bit of impatience in her voice said, "You know that God will take care of you, even in a thunderstorm."

The child paused for a skeptical moment and said,

"Yes, but when it's thundering and lightning I need somebody to love me who has skin on."

God came into the midst of the storm of our sinfulness in the Person of Jesus Christ. In his humanity, the Savior is God with skin on.

All of us want to be loved—not only with words, but with practical and, sometimes, physical expressions of that mysterious inner feeling. When my job requires me to be away from my wife, our daily phone calls are valuable expressions of love and caring. But they cannot compare to the enjoyment of being with each other.

If love is an important ingredient of life, even when things are going smoothly, it is indispensable for those who are going through dark periods of distress.

It isn't enough simply to remind troubled people that God loves them. The New Testament Book of James teaches that faith which does not result in helpful action is dead.

"My brothers, what good is it for someone to say that he has faith if his actions do not prove it? Can that faith save him? Suppose there are brothers and sisters who need clothes and don't have enough to eat. What good is there in your saying to them, 'God bless you! Keep warm and eat well!'—if you don't give them the necessities of life? So it is with faith: if it is alone and has no actions with it, then it is dead" (James 2:14–17, TEV).

It is only when expressions such as "God loves you" are accompanied by practical follow-through that they are part of a balanced ministry.

I can vouch for the value of practical expressions of concern.

Since many people in my circle of acquaintance couldn't handle a "distress situation" that occurred during a dark period in my life, they withdrew and became quite busy with their own concerns until the storm was over. A few were able to hang in there with me, knowing my need for love with skin on. It didn't take much—a phone call or letter now and then. But those expressions provided some stability which helped me get life back on course.

The Bible teaches that believers have a unique opportunity to be the avenues of God's love with skin on.

Some situations naturally lend themselves to a ministering response.

One Monday I turned on the early morning news and heard that a four-year-old girl from the next town was lost. Little Susan Parr had not come home for dinner the night before. Her frantic parents and neighbors searched the nearby woods until dark without finding a trace of her. The next morning authorities were appealing for volunteers to join in the search.

I went to the gathering site and joined hundreds of other people in a human chain line, checking the woods foot by foot.

Several hours later, word came that Susan had been found. She was asleep under a bush, unharmed.

The community responded to the emergency admirably. Businesses closed, and people stayed home from work and school so that they could help.

It is natural to respond to the plight of parents of

a lost child, or a friend who has an incurable disease. These difficulties, which are beyond the personal control of the individuals involved, cause us to give all the support we can muster.

But, when we suspect that the individual may, at least in part, be responsible for causing his own problems, it is more difficult to be sympathetic. Embezzlement, marriage failure, divorce or drug and alcohol abuse involve a certain amount of personal decision and will.

In some circles these manifestations of need are simplistically dismissed as the fruit of personal sin alone. As a result there is a tendency to withdraw from people who are trying to cope with these deeply wounding experiences. This reluctance to help is based on the idea that "they got themselves into this mess, they can get themselves out of it."

I recently received a letter from a religious organization telling of the "mutually agreed upon resignation" of an employee due to his "marital problems." I knew that the employee was dedicated and well respected for his work.

Since I went through a similar separation from a religious organization, I knew that the wording of the letter was probably a public relations method of saying, "He was fired because we were afraid of what our constituency might say if they found out about his marriage difficulties." In my opinion, this action is a contradiction of the Christian faith.

In both cases, the forced resignations came about not out of concern for individuals who were hurting severely, but out of fear of possible revenue losses. It seems to me that this is like kicking a man while he is down. It is withdrawing support from an individual when he needs it most.

This attitude is foreign to the ministry of Jesus. In one story he told about a shepherd who left ninety-nine safe sheep to search for one which was lost. There is no indication that the shepherd said, "He is a stupid sheep and repeatedly wanders off by himself. I want nothing more to do with him. Let him find his own way back if he can." No, as soon as the shepherd discovered that one of his sheep was missing he instantly, without consideration of causes, set out to find his distressed lamb and bring him back.

Sometimes, long-term pressures build and cause life to veer from its normal course. Unresolved conflicts and long-suppressed frustrations rise to the surface and throw life out of balance.

We can provide a stabilizing ministry to people who may be going through a personal hell, regardless of the cause, if we will adopt the following guidelines.

1. *Resist the urge to assign blame.*

"Who sinned, this man, or his parents, that he was born blind?" With this question to Jesus, his disciples showed the human tendency to assign blame.

Jesus' answer indicated that their question was irrelevant. The important issue was the man's condition, not who was to blame for it. He was hurting and needed help.

While the disciples were occupied with fixing responsibility, Jesus was concerned with fixing blind eyes.

There is a sharp difference between placing blame and determining causes. Blame implies judgment and is almost always destructive to relationships. Attempting to understand causes indicates a constructive desire to help.

It is not always possible to fathom the long-term, complex pressures which have led to a person's distress. The individual himself is probably unaware of all of the unresolved tensions which have built up inside him.

I have a friend whose personality used to repel people. She was sharp-tongued and often lashed out at others unnecessarily. She developed serious physical problems which eventually led to a stay in the hospital.

After a series of counseling sessions, her doctor was able to diagnose the cause of her difficulties. Her tendency to lash out and her physical illnesses were manifestations of years of supressed conflict caused by an unsatisfactory marriage. When she was able to resolve her marital problems, the unpleasant results of her tension disappeared.

More often than not, in our ordinary personal ministries we have to be content to say, "I don't understand the contributing factors, but I want to help if I can."

Determining the real reasons for situations such as alcoholism, drug addiction, or marriage failure is best left to professionals.

In the case of a divorce it is easy to fall into the trap of branding one partner "innocent" and the other "guilty." There then follows the inclination to minister to the "innocent" and ignore or condemn the "guilty." When one partner leaves home, his or her "guilt" is usually assumed. However, the person who remains may have created an intolerable atmosphere, forcing the mate to leave in order to survive.

A "guilty" person may be the one whose imperfections are most open to public scrutiny. Years of private sinning against his or her personality by the "innocent" partner may have gone publicly unnoticed.

Professional counselors indicate that rarely is one party completely innocent and the other completely guilty.

(A word of caution: unless you are professionally trained, do not allow yourself to try to "straighten out" someone else's marital problems. That kind of involvement will usually make the situation worse.)

Several years ago I met a lady who was well on her way to becoming an alcoholic. Because she smelled of liquor, even early in the morning, I was repelled by her. I regret that my reaction was negative. Judgmentally, I thought, "Why would she allow herself to get into this condition?"

Over the months that followed I learned about some of the enormous pressures that built up in her life. Apparently her drinking helps her escape from those pressures for a little while.

Who sinned, this lady or someone else, that she has a drinking problem? The question, like that of the disciples, is irrelevant. The need is for a healing, supportive personal ministry.

When we overcome the urge to assign blame, we

are better prepared to minister to people who need to put their lives back into balance.

2. *Learn to distinguish between appearance and reality.*

Mathematically, two plus two always equals four. Unfortunately, this formula cannot always be applied when adding up apparent "facts" about people. Things are not always what they appear to be on the surface. Many false conclusions are drawn based only on what people see and hear.

Appearance. The wife of a United States President occasionally walked through the halls of the White House in an erratic manner.

False Conclusion. Based on what they saw, several reporters published a story that she was an alcoholic.

Reality. The real cause of her problem was an inner ear disorder which made it difficult for her to maintain balance.

Remember that a placid, serene public appearance may be hiding a deeply troubled spirit. A seemingly "perfect" marriage may subtly contain festering, unresolved conflicts in one or both partners.

When you are close enough to have direct conversation with individuals who are hurting, realize that they are telling you their truth as they see it. People enduring distress sometimes erect strong defenses to avoid further hurt. An individual who is struggling for survival may find it necessary to change the rules under which he or she normally operates in order to get through the crisis period.

A person who is temporarily locked into a critical test of his or her lifestyle will experience a degree of shock, and possibly guilt. These feelings have a distorting effect on personal objectivity.

The stories that are spawned around any personal crisis are usually accompanied by exaggeration and false conclusions which can cause permanent damage to people's lives. We may learn some unsavory facts about other people. But the mere knowledge that something is true does not obligate us to share it with others if it can cause further discomfort.

Try, as best you can, to sift away the appearances and aim for an understanding of the reality and truth involved.

3. *Show your compassion by helping people face reality.*

Compassion has two sides. Its soft side is the initial, sympathetic response which causes us to reach out to a person who is hurting. Its hard side is the sometimes painful experience of helping people face reality.

The troubled individual who is constantly shown the soft side of compassion may develop a debilitating dependency on other people. When our initial sympathetic reaction is combined with efforts to help a person accept his real situation, he is encouraged to stand on his own feet and deal with his difficulties constructively.

It is true that God has the power to cure an alcoholic instantly. But the afflicted person must also realistically face the option that his road to relief may be long and difficult, requiring outside help.

An embezzler may find hope in the idea that God can miraculously remove the consequences of his thievery. But he should also be prepared to suffer the penalty for his acts, should God choose not to intervene.

The person whose marriage partner has left may properly be encouraged to pray that God will cause him or her to return. But compassionate friends should also help that individual reconstruct life in light of the possibility that the partner might not come back.

When we minister to people by helping them face reality we have encouraged the first step toward bringing their lives back into harmony.

In John 8, the incident of an adulterous woman brought before Jesus, the brilliance of his God-with-skin-on ministry shines in contrast to the dark attitudes of her accusers.

Displaying the human tendency to make a public spectacle of other people's sins, they dragged her to Jesus in front of a huge crowd, unconcerned about her embarrassment.

The ever-compassionate Christ, however, did not even address himself to the woman until the crowd dispersed and they were alone.

Her accusers brought her to Jesus as a test case, hoping to bolster their sagging religious-legal-moral system. But Jesus, knowing that systems were made for man and not man for systems, put her needs and feelings first.

The religious leaders judged her sins to be worse than the sins of others.

Jesus made it clear that sins of hypocrisy and lack

of compassion are on an equal par with her sin. Sins are sins regardless of the form they take. None are any worse or better than others.

The people who brought this woman to Jesus were prone to dismiss years of past success and future potential to exact their pound of flesh for an isolated failure. On the other hand, Jesus saw her worth, and saved her for her future.

The world still has more than its share of the attitudes of the accusers. The need is for God-with-skin-on personal ministries based on the attitudes of Jesus Christ.

You can have that kind of ministry.

4. More Assets than Moses

Discovering Resources for Ministering

You say, "But I'm so ordinary that I don't have anything to offer in ministry to others"?

Nonsense. Everybody was created with a capacity to share some ministering gift. God certainly did not skip you in the process.

This frustrating feeling of ordinariness has a long history. Even Moses felt that he did not have much to offer. When God told him that he had been selected to lead the Israelites to freedom he replied, "Who am I?" He might also have said, "Lord, you must have set the wrong bush on fire. What do I have to offer? Look at my past. Have you forgotten how my wild temper made a murderer out of me? Haven't you heard my 'spiritual' friends who tell me that you can never use me again because of that tragedy forty years ago? Besides, look at me now—just an ordinary, eighty-year-old shepherd. I'm not persuasive and I'm a terrible public speaker. Nobody will listen to me. You need somebody who is more spectacular."

Talk about a poor self-image!

But God knew that Moses had accumulated a whole arsenal of ordinary resources—his experiences, his personality, and even his shepherd's rod. And God would use these resources in an extraordinary way.

Imagine how "ordinary" Moses felt about his sheepherding experience on the back side of the desert. Forty years of nothing but sand and those dumb sheep. Sand and sheep . . . sand and sheep. How ordinary can you get?

But think of the benefits he gained! He learned the rudiments of survival in the desert—devising ways to provide food and clothing for his family, escaping the devastating effects of the scorching heat, guarding against the bone-chilling curtain of cold that suddenly drops on the desert at nightfall. Endurance, patience, physical conditioning . . .

All of these assets, gained from ordinary experiences, equipped Moses to minister to the homeless sheep of Israel as he led them through the desert to the promised land.

Examine the list of Jesus' disciples. What do you see? Any religious leaders? Any public speakers? Any gifted singers? Anybody with spectacular talent? No. Ordinary, everyday people. Fishermen and a tax-collector.

Chances are that your formal education is more complete than that of Moses or any of the disciples. You undoubtedly have many more material possessions.

These are resources which you can use in ministering to other people.

What do you have to offer?

First, you have *yourself.*

With a personality that shows cheerful, contagious friendliness, you can minister to people every day.

I boarded a city transit bus during rush hour and listened as the driver received numerous complaints about being late. (The traffic had been unusually heavy that morning.) It was easy to see that his patience was quickly coming to an end. At one crowded stop, a lady with a charming smile got on and greeted him with, "Good morning, how are you today, John?" That small bit of inexpensive courtesy seemed to help him regain his composure, as he responded, "Fine, thank you."

You don't have to be spectacular to open your personality and share genuine cheerfulness with people whose services are taken for granted. Consistently giving some friendliness to a waitress, postman, or toll collector may open opportunities for further ministry and witness.

With your ears you can perform the ministry of listening for someone who needs a sympathetic, understanding friend.

You can train your eyes to look for signs of need—a sad face, a tearful eye, or a disruption in routine which may indicate that someone is having difficulty.

You can minister with your mouth by learning to speak or remain silent at the appropriate times—and you can always form it into a smile.

You can use your hands to write letters, do chores,

or change dressings for a person who is recovering from surgery.

Your feet can carry you on countless errands of concern and care.

Even though you may not think that you have unusual talent, you do have your personality, your ears, eyes, mouth, hands, and feet. These are your most important ministering assets. You can use them to help people who need you.

Second in your inventory of ministering resources, you have *your accumulated experiences.* Successes and failures have taught you lessons which you could not have learned from books. These experiences uniquely equip you to minister to people who may be going through similar times of trial or triumph.

You may have faced difficult physical, emotional, business, or marriage situations in your own life. The wisdom which you have gained can provide valuable help to others. The fact that "you have been there" opens the door to minister to people who are "there now."

I once read of a woman who lost all of her possessions in a devastating fire. Because of that experience she became especially sensitive to others who had the same misfortune. Whenever such an incident was reported in the newspaper she contacted the family involved and offered her assistance. She made some lasting friendships and found unique opportunities to minister because she had "been there" and understood.

For several years I was part of an adult study group. About fifteen people participated in the weekly sessions.

One evening the question for discussion was, "When did you experience the most significant spiritual growth and what caused it?"

Each person answered with a situation of pain, problems with children, financial crisis, marriage conflict, or the death of someone close. It was apparent that these difficult times had provided the impetus toward unprecedented spiritual maturing in each person's life.

Everyone present testified that these difficulties had equipped them with greater understanding and compassion for ministering to other people.

I learned a similar lesson as a result of several periods as a hospital patient. I noticed that my prayers were different while I was in the hospital. They were more honest and to the point. I began to write them down.

> "Lord, I've always said that I believed a lot of things about you. But some of those things were never very real because they were just words. Now I'm being tested. And, I'm finding that some of the things that I've talked about really work. I'm also aware that I've done a lot of pretending.
>
> "Take away the pretense and make me honest with you—and with myself. Thank you for the strengthening of belief that comes with this kind of testing."

This and several other prayers that grew out of my hospital experiences have been published under the title, *As You Recover.** I'm happy that the booklet has received wide distribution and is now helping other people who are hospitalized. This is a ministry which I could not have had without my firsthand experience as a patient.

And so, in addition to your physical assets, you can also use your experiences to minister to other people. Everything that you have learned can be shared to assist some other person.

Third in your list of ministering assets, include *your material possessions.*

Our insurance agent has encouraged us to inventory all of the things that we own. He said, "Don't overlook even the smallest item. In case of a loss, most people underestimate the number and value of what they possess."

I suspect that the same is true when we inventory our tools for ministry.

Your home is probably your most valuable material possession—and it can be your most useful ministering asset.

Eddie and Margie Allen have continually welcomed needy people into the warm, healing comfort of their home. Over the years countless people who were alone, confused, shaken, or ill have found the Allen house to be a place to put things back together. Whenever I walk through the back door I think of how the place has been used to provide a ministry of stability. People

---

* Grand Rapids: Baker Book House.

have come in a state of despair and have left, sometimes months later, having recovered perspective and strength.

You too can provide hospitality in your home for lonely people—either with a meal, or an extended period of recovery.

With your car you can provide transportation to church, to the hospital, or to the store as the needs arise. There may be some people near you who will find a simple ride in the country to be a welcome, ministering change from boredom and loneliness.

Use your telephone to contact an elderly person regularly so that the individual will know that someone cares.

Soon after we moved into a new neighborhood we met our delightful neighbor. She is a vivacious and active retired school teacher. She lives alone. After our telephone was installed she asked for our number. "I would like to have it in case I have an emergency sometime. Then I know that I can get help," she said.

If having her neighbor's telephone number is important to an active lady in her seventies, think how valuable regular phone contact must be to an older person who is shut in. This brief contact with the outside world can provide some much needed security.

Think how you can assist people who are in need with your washing machine, stove, sewing machine, iron, tools, typewriter, buckets and detergent. These are not pulpits or pianos. But they *are* possessions with which you can minister to needy people all around you.

I know several widows, past retirement age, living on fixed incomes. They may be forced, reluctantly, to leave their homes. Not because of big expenditures, but because they cannot afford to hire people to perform routine maintenance chores to keep their houses functioning well.

Cleaning rain gutters, cutting the grass, repairing a leaky toilet valve, replacing worn-out faucet washers—routine work for most men—seem like overwhelming obstacles to a widow who must hire someone to do them.

A man, or group of men, can perform vital ministries with their tools—ministries which may make it possible for an elderly woman living alone to stay in the home that she loves.

These ordinary assets can be used to reach out. When you add them up, you will discover that you probably have more to offer than Moses or any of the disciples. Nothing spectacular. Nothing unusual. But ordinary tools, for ordinary people, which can be used to develop extraordinary ministries.

5. Freeing the Flow

Removing Hindrances to Ministering

Have you heard the story about a clergyman visiting a hospitalized parishioner? Shortly after the minister arrived, the patient, who was receiving oxygen, began having severe breathing difficulty. His concerned pastor asked, "Can I do something to help you?" The patient gasped, "Yes, get off my air hose!"

As a special creation of God, you are gifted with a capacity to minister to people. In addition to your capabilities you may also have an awakening desire to reach out to those who need you.

But, the flow of our unique abilities is often interrupted by attitudes which cut off the air supply necessary for effective personal ministering. Freeing that flow requires the removal of ministry-quenching encumbrances. We need to be sure that our attitudes are not causing us to stand on our own air hoses.

I don't know what those hindrances may be for you, but I can share what some of mine have been.

Guilt

"If you persist in the path you have chosen you will never again be used by God as a blessing to others."

Those words of judgment were said to me when I was going through the most difficult situation that I had ever faced—a family break-up. To make matters worse, they came from a person who had a reputation for being a great "prayer warrior and biblical scholar."

I spent several months at the bottom of the pit of despair, thinking that, at age forty-two, my useful life of ministry was over. This feeling of uselessness stemmed from guilt—some real, much imposed by other people. As a result, I resigned myself to a life of meaningless, menial tasks.

The removal of this ministry-thwarting burden of unresolved guilt came in four ways.

First, I began to study the lives of biblical personalities.

Although there is a tendency to attribute a semidivine nature to the "greats" of the Bible—as if they did not have the same human frame as ours—I discovered that some of the most effective leaders were people who had suffered enormous personal failure.

Who could deny that Moses was used by God as one of the most effective political and spiritual leaders of all time?

And yet, in his younger years, he murdered a man. His escape into the desert, the long years in seclusion, and his evident inferiority complex probably grew out of guilt over his failures.

David has been castigated for his sins of adultery

and secondhand murder. But his Psalms, many of which grew out of those humanizing experiences, have helped millions of people in times of distress.

Peter's three-time denial of Christ on the night before the crucifixion did not exclude him from further usefulness in the kingdom of God. His subsequent bold acts of faith in the early development of the church continue to inspire us today.

These fellow human beings sinned and failed. But, more important, they experienced God's forgiveness and guilt-removing grace. They went on to develop personal ministries appropriate to their capabilities.

I came to believe that God would do the same for me. And, he has.

Second, I listened to a recording by Mike Warnke,* a former Satanist priest who is now a Christian. Mike ministered to me with a new appreciation of God, the Perfect Forgetter. He said, "You can ask God to forgive you for something and he forgives you. You can come back five minutes later and say, 'Lord, do you remember that thing that I just asked forgiveness for?' and he'll answer, 'No.' It's not even on the account books any more."

Because of the Grace of God, my confessions bring his forgiveness and remove my guilt as if the sins never existed.

Some people find it hard to forgive. Others are not inclined to let me forget the past. But, I thank God that there is nothing that I have ever done, or will

---

* *Mike Warnke Live*, Myrrh/Word, MSA 6561.

ever do, that is beyond his Perfect Forgetting. He doesn't even remember what other people may continue to bring up about my forgiven sins.

Once these lessons became a part of me I stopped berating myself for things that I couldn't change. I still have my capabilities—and there are still ministries to be carried out.

Third, through reading the book, *When I Say No I Feel Guilty*,* I realized that I allowed myself, even in the most intimate relationships, to be manipulated by subtle appeals to my guilt feelings. It was my own fault that I allowed this to happen.

The statement "If you persist in the path you have chosen you will never again be used as a blessing to others" is an example of a pious attempt to manipulate through an appeal of guilt. At the time I did not recognize it as a guilt-producing attempt to maneuver me into a course of action which was more acceptable to the speaker. Instead, I succumbed to the imposed guilt, became depressed, and thus, ineffective.

Now that I understand better what happened, I can guard against the encumbrance of manipulative guilt.

Fourth, it is refreshing to be in a new church where the pastor presents the warmth of the Gospel.

Each Sunday after a unison prayer of confession, he assures us that we stand forgiven and freed from guilt in Jesus Christ. This week-by-week reminder has contributed immensely to my growing appreciation of the Grace of God.

---

* Manuel J. Smith (New York: Bantam Books, 1975).

For too much of my life I allowed guilt feelings to rob me of the opportunity to reach out with my full potential. Nagging feelings of unresolved guilt led to a loss of self-worth. And a low level of self-esteem slows the flow of personal ministry.

Now I can see that some of the Christian service in which I have been involved grew out of guilt motivation. In my high school and college years speakers reminded us that thousands of people were dying without Christ each day. It was our responsibility to reach those lost souls. We were urged to enter "full-time" Christian service. Underneath was a subtle implication—"If you don't, then you will have to carry the responsibility for all of those who are lost." An appeal to guilt! And some of us entered "full-time" ministries for that reason.

There is an exciting difference emerging now. My personal ministries are not based on what I can do to or for other people. They grow out of what I am becoming as a person.

From my present perspective, the former ways of ministering seem forced and artificial. The new way is more natural and, I believe, more effective.

The Approval-Rejection Syndrome

I have always wanted people to like me. I guess everybody does. For most of my life I found my sense of worth in what other people thought of me.

As a result, I tried to project the image that they—my wife, my employer, my fellow church members—

expected of me. Because I was fairly successful at this charade, people seemed to like me most of the time.

But, while gaining the respect and acceptance of others, I grew to dislike and reject myself. I knew I was not being me. The repeated sacrifice of one's true self to the expectations of other people leads to a decline in self-value. And when that happens, all the other relationships begin to disintegrate.

I stood in the waiting room of a small train station in New Jersey, ready to board the express to New York City. An antique wood stove provided the waiting passengers with a warm refuge from the cold, January wind.

Since the express was late, I watched several local commuter trains arrive, fill with passengers, and depart. On one occasion, a would-be rider rushed down the platform just in time to miss his connection. Frustrated, he burst into the waiting room, uttered a few choice four-letter words, kicked the stove and then decided to go outside in the cold until the next train arrived.

Friends of mine, Bob and Becky Hight, have at times, like the stove in the train station, been kicked unjustly by people to whom they have extended their care. But they radiate a warm, understanding love that is not conditioned by a desire for approval or the fear of rejection, and their example has helped me grow out of the approval-rejection syndrome.

Even when their love has been rejected and those to whom it was offered choose to stand outside in the cold, my friends continue to pour out their warmth. They manage to keep their door open so that those who have temporarily rejected their love can walk back into the circle of care when they choose to do so.

That kind of love is not easy. Sometimes it hurts. But it is not encumbered by the approval-rejection syndrome. And this frees the flow of some unique personal ministries for Bob and Becky.

Man-made Religion

On a visit to the Southwest I looked out of my hotel window to a contrasting vista of the temporary and the permanent. Close at hand was the gaudy Las Vegas Strip, lined with gambling casinos—each with its own man-made style of overdone opulence. In the distance stood the rugged Nevada mountain country—a paradox of barren beauty.

The useful life-span of those buildings is short when compared with the endurance of the mountainous creations of God.

Jesus' life was a contention between the temporary and the permanent. In his human nature he was the Perfect Example of freedom. He willingly bound himself in obedience to his Father. But he was in continuing conflict with the restrictive, man-made system taught by the religionists of his day.

The fundamental law of God was designed to create the conditions for human fulfillment. But religious leaders added hundreds of minute rules of their own. Religion became too ponderous and burdensome for the average person. Jesus strongly denounced those who turned the freeing avenues of God into a spiritual dead-end by adding their own detours.

Similar situations still exist. During my teenage years, youth group leaders and conference speakers reminded us that "Christians shouldn't dance, drink, smoke, play cards, or go to the movies." The judgment that anyone who indulged in these things couldn't possibly be a Christian was implied. My conclusion then? I had better comply with the accepted "Christian" behavior code if I wanted people to know that I was a believer.

This message was pounded home so often, usually with out-of-context biblical support, that these man-made rules took on a certain divine sound. They became mixed up with the principles of God.

Some religious groups unintentionally create their own exclusive subculture. They gradually develop rules for the behavior of their members. Occasionally these rules are written, but most of the time they are "understood." To remain a member of the fellowship, in good standing, one must adhere to these expansions on the law of God. Nonconformity usually brings judgment, and sometimes ostracism.

In a few churches, "shunning" is used as an official method of discipline. A nonconforming church member may be subjected to social isolation by his family, friends, and business associates until he "repents." Even though this is not an official practice in most church organizations, it often exists in the form of group attitudes and "Christian" peer pressure.

I have been associated with movements which attempted to create hundreds of faceless conformists who would respond to life situations in a programmed manner. This is unbiblical and unnatural. It robs people of their uniqueness and their rightful freedom. It also tends to reduce the flexibility necessary for effective personal ministering.

I believe that I am learning to sift the temporary additions of men from the permanent, freedom-giving principles of God. As I become more adept at separating the two, my personal ministry opportunities expand.

Personal Inertia

It was an early October afternoon. I stopped in Portland, Maine, for a few hours of business. Then, I planned to move on to Auburn, the next city on my itinerary.

The wind had a cool, biting edge as the shadows of the office buildings lengthened toward evening. I thought, "Four months from now, when I make my next visit here, it will be bitter cold." Already the natives had put away their summer clothes and were pulling overcoat collars up around their necks as they walked along Congress Street.

On my way toward the parking lot I noticed a tall man in his thirties bending over one of the trash containers that is strategically placed every half block. He did not look like a shabby derelict, though his appearance showed signs that his resources might have run out.

He sifted through the receptacle vigorously while scores of unnoticing people walked by. From the can he pulled a familiar Styrofoam box containing the remains of a cold, partially eaten "Big Mac." He sniffed it as if to test its suitability, then swallowed someone else's garbage. I thought I was going to be sick.

For a moment I felt his humiliation and wanted to reach out to him. Then, my excuses began their invasion.

> "Maybe he's an alcoholic—if I give him money he'll probably spend it on drink."
>
> "There must be other places where he can go for help."
>
> "Somebody else will help him. After all, I'm just passing through town. It's not my responsibility."
>
> "The city must have a welfare program that can assist him."
>
> "Maybe he's lazy—he probably brought his problems on himself."

Rapid-fire excuses—one after another.

Finally, piercing through all of the rationalizations came the words, "He's hungry. Feed him."

But by then, it was too late. The opportunity, and the man, had disappeared.

This missed ministry opportunity would not have required special talent or unusual ability—just a few seconds of time and several dollars—both of which I could spare.

And I prayed, "Lord, forgive me for being too careful about reaching out. Help me to be more quickly responsive to needs like this."

I believe that the memory of this missed opportunity will help me overcome my natural reluctance to reach out to others in need.

I regret that it took me so many years to identify these hindrances to my personal ministry—guilt, the approval-rejection syndrome, man-made religion, and personal inertia. But I am grateful that, at last, I am being freed to a broader effectiveness.

What may be thwarting you in your personal outreach? Once you are able to get off your own air hose, you will experience the exhilaration of becoming a natural ministry to others, not so much by what you do, but by what you are.

6. "NOBODY WEARS SHOES"

Recognizing Opportunities for Ministering

I was glad that the Boeing 747 was nearly empty as we took off from Chicago. In my state of mind I didn't want to be bothered talking to anyone. The plane touched down at McCarren Airport in Las Vegas several minutes ahead of schedule.

In just under four hours it had torn me, alone and out of work, away from everything that had grown familiar to me. As the miles passed rapidly, I was conscious that valued relationships were fading—most, never to be resumed again.

The barren, desert surroundings of my new "home" somehow matched the parched feeling inside of me. The unnerving suddenness of this transfer presented me with unexpected cultural shock.

Over the years I had built all of my relationships with people of similar beliefs. I had worked for a religious publishing company and associated with

Christians in business. Social contacts were almost exclusively with Christians.

Now, I was suddenly wrenched out of the safe environment which I had built. I had to cope with the real world of people who had not yet discovered the benefits of being Christian—nor did they seem to care to.

Along with its difficulties, which were many, this change in culture had its advantages.

First, I discovered the exhilaration of being released from bondage to the opinions of other people. Here, in my new surroundings, I found that I was accepted at face value as a person. I was not expected to be a behavior pattern for others.

My college education included two years of compulsory ROTC military training. We were exposed to the rudiments of marching, the care and use of the M-1 rifle (rendered inoperative by its missing firing pin) and, above all, military appearance. I once had the "honor" of being selected "Cadet of the Week." This meant that, at least for one week, I was the epitome of what a military cadet should be. I had executed the marching steps with precision. My uniform was pressed and polished to perfection. The M-1 was clean and functioning (as well as a rifle without its firing pin can function).

An elaborate system of demerits had been devised to help cadets see the wisdom of abiding by the rules. Infractions of the rules led to the assignment of demerits which had to be worked off through extra projects.

We were continually reminded that all of these activities helped to broaden the base of our national military preparedness. Maybe so. But by the end of the first year I had come to dislike every moment given to marching, polishing, pressing, and rifle-cleaning. It all seemed so artificial.

Much the same feeling had grown inside of me as I continued in my safe, Christian culture. I realized that I had fallen into the trap of keeping my spiritual buttons polished so that I would "pass muster" with my Christian friends. This feeling, always being on parade, always feeling responsible for the actions of other people, can turn one slightly paranoid.

I longed to become an authentic person—to share my weaknesses and my doubts as well as my strengths and beliefs. But I knew that such behavior would be unacceptable and would win me an overwhelming burden of demerits from my peers.

Now, in my new environment, there was none of that. The feeling of being freed from bondage to the opinions of other people is akin to the joy that I found on the day that the compulsory military training was over. I was first in line to hand in my uniform and rifle. I haven't missed them one bit.

Second, being transplanted into a new environment opened my eyes to ministry opportunities that I had not seen before. Firsthand I learned the truth of Jesus' statement, "Lift up your eyes unto the fields, for they are already white unto harvest." My previous small world had become sterile and ingrown—it had desensitized me to the needs of people outside my tightly drawn circle of acquaintances.

I moved my few personal belongings into a cramped, two-room apartment in a twenty-four-unit complex just one block from the famous Las Vegas Strip. The swimming pool and other appointments indicated that the building once was first-class. Now, there were telltale signs of creeping tackiness which would soon bring it to a point of no return.

Since the door of each apartment opened onto a central courtyard, I was able to sit at poolside and observe my privacy-guarding neighbors come and go.

Sometimes I was overwhelmed with the opportunities for ministry that began to emerge. I thought of the prominent shoe manufacturing company which sent a fledgling salesman to the heart of Africa to test his sales ability. After one month he wired the home office saying, "Coming home. No opportunity here; nobody wears shoes." The company sent another man. After two weeks he wired the home office and said, "Great opportunity here. Nobody wears shoes. Everybody is a prospect."

Everybody that I met in my new location seemed to be a prospect for some form of ministry.

Dotty, in her mid-fifties, had lived in apartment number 6 since the complex opened fifteen years earlier. She had the repelling demeanor of an angry drill sergeant—perhaps a carryover from her stint in the WACS during World War II. I suspected that her surly bossiness was a self-protective device which had helped her survive for so long in a town where human values are scarce.

She started each day by swallowing a stiff whiskey sour. At 3:00 P.M. Dotty drove her 1968 Chevy, transmission fluid trailing behind her, to the hotel where she worked as a telephone reservations clerk.

Aside from her constant companionship with a can of beer and a rasping cough, she was alone.

Ninety-year-old Mrs. Ashton occupied number 16. She was from Israel and spoke very little English. Since she was a smoker, we all feared that she might fall asleep with a lighted cigarette and set the building on fire. Several strokelike seizures had distorted her face and caused her to lean to the left as she walked. She tottered dangerously close to the pool when she moved through the courtyard.

She too, was alone—and probably frightened.

Each night from 10:00 P.M. until 4:00 A.M. Brian, number 7, sat expressionless as he played his drums in smoke-filled cocktail lounges. Twenty years in the same routine had made him cynical and jaded. In spite of the fact that he always seemed to be at odds with his employer and fellow musicians, he never lacked work—perhaps because he was a good drummer, or, more likely, because he knew the right people.

Brian exhibited a suspicious, robotlike detachment from other people. He was a loner.

The attractive singer in number 14 was billed as Tania Styles. Offstage she looked like any other twenty-four-year-old girl in jeans and sweat shirt. But her transformed, on-stage appearance was something to behold. She took on the delightful beauty of slightly understated elegance and became the envy of the other lady performers.

Tania's professional talent could lead her to stardom. She already enjoyed the applause of audiences in some of the best night spots in town. She had class, spirit, and high ideals. But behind the staged smile and studied gestures, she cautiously reached out of her aloneness.

Dawn, barely twenty-one, rented apartment number 2. She was one of over 2500 prostitutes who operated "illegally" but openly in the county. More than one million tourists and conventioneers who visited the town each year provided these "working girls" with plenty of opportunity. With the "right" connections a girl could earn as much as $100,000 per year, tax free. Without the "right" contacts, the clientele was undesirable and the earnings poor. Dawn did not have the "right" connections. In spite of the steady flow of men to her door, her expression betrayed emptiness and boredom.

Carlton Shepherd, an accomplished pianist, was the most successful entertainer in the building. His group was always in demand. Working until almost sunrise, he slept only a few hours each day. Extra "gigs" kept him occupied in the early evening before his regular "sets" began. His wife, Sharon, had been seriously ill in the hospital. Carlton was having a hard time caring for the two children by himself. He needed help.

Martha, her invalid brother, and her mentally disturbed son lived in number 8. They came from Italy and spoke broken English. Their constant bickering was heard throughout the complex. Martha worked hard as a seamstress—but had no one who would take the time to try to understand her attempts to communicate.

What did all of this mean? Simply this. There is no lack of opportunities for personal ministry. The limitations which we see are largely self-imposed.

It is easy for us to withdraw into the safety of our Christian community and lose the vision of sharing ourselves and our faith with those who really need it. Sometimes, in the name of "separation," we build walls to protect ourselves from ugly realities. This is like a group of firemen declaring that they will remain in the firehouse because they do not like acrid smoke and intense heat.

Want a place to begin? Look for someone who is alone; someone who is overlooked because of a physical, mental or emotional handicap; someone who is shunned because of a "different" life style; someone who is alienated because of sin. These are the people to whom Jesus ministered.

Shake off the comfortableness of your closed Christian community. Look around you . . . look next door

. . . look across the street . . . look at the real world of people.

Put yourself in the mainstream where people live—the needs will cascade around you. Each one is an opportunity for your ministry.

7. A Washing Machine and Valentine Candy

Establishing Relationships for Ministering

As I got acquainted with my new neighbors, it seemed to me that the hot, stinging desert wind often blew their values away at will. For many of them, survival was the name of the game. Most people appeared to be barely enduring life. Some of this I attributed to the ovenlike, 115-degree temperatures.

In contrast, Cathy and Scott Bowen, who lived in apartment number 22, exhibited a refreshing stability and enjoyment of life. It hadn't taken long for me to sense that they were different—not strange, odd, or repulsive—but pleasantly different. After several days I noticed that the lonely people in my small apartment world were mysteriously drawn to the Bowens, though neither of them made any obvious efforts to reach out.

The first indication of this came one Sunday afternoon when Martha, our Italian neighbor, came out to the pool looking very concerned. Cathy's sensitivity detected her distress immediately. Calmly she said, "Martha, you seem troubled." She then listened patiently as Martha tried to explain that her brother was seriously ill but was afraid to go to the doctor. Martha didn't know what to do.

Cathy and Scott were able to help Martha out of her dilemma by securing the telephone number of a twenty-four-hour family medical service. Martha took the information and got the necessary help for her brother.

After that, whenever Cathy was at poolside, I noticed that Martha would stop by to chat. She had found someone in this strange country who would take the time to listen, even though it was hard work. Several times I overheard them talking about what it means to be a Christian.

For months, Dawn occasionally poked her head out of her darkened apartment to blink briefly at the sunlight. If no one was in sight she would step out onto the balcony to bask in the fresh air.

I learned that shortly after Cathy and Scott arrived on the scene, Dawn seemed to make a special effort to come outside between customers, wave and cast a wistful look at the couple beside the pool. She sensed from their cheery nonjudgmental, "How are you, Dawn?" that they cared—and that they were not the kind of people who would take advantage of her.

The American Bible Society has prepared a version of *Good News for Modern Man* for distribution to people in show business. The cover is a collage of entertainment billboards featuring the names of famous stars.

Scott noticed Carlton Shepherd's name under a headliner on the back cover. Carlton was quite amused to find his name on the cover of a Bible. When Scott offered a copy to him, he said, "I've always wanted to read that book. Sure I'll take it."

Dotty used her hostility to keep people at arm's length. She didn't want to be likable. But a change began with Cathy's simple question, "Dotty, I'm having trouble with the apartment washing machine. Would you please show me how to use it properly?" (Everybody likes to be asked for advice.) This encounter was short and grumpy. But, with persistent friendliness, Dotty began to melt. On Valentine's Day I was surprised to see her walk across the courtyard, beer can in hand, knock on the door of number 22 and hand Cathy and Scott a Valentine card and some candy. She was reaching out for the first time in years.

As time went on, Scott and Cathy did make a conscious effort to reach Brian. One evening they visited the lounge where he played his drums. (Apparently they had outgrown the tendency to worry about what other people might think about them if they were seen going into such a place.) This time they tried to let Brian know that they cared. For an hour their smiles were met with his vacant, jaded stare. Finally, his eyes opened wide and a shy smile cracked across his face—his first in several months. He even managed a half-hearted nod as they rose to leave.

Call these beginnings what you will—human courtesy . . . pre-evangelism . . . Christian concern. The important fact is that the positive pole of Cathy and

Scott's caring combined with the negative pole of their neighbors' needs to create a magnetic situation. This is the way relationships are established. And when that happens, the potential for sharing the Gospel increases. There is no way to foresee how the Holy Spirit will make these seeds blossom.

The Bowens did not exhibit spectacular talents or abilities. They were ordinary people, like you and me. But they had a profound ministering influence. They did what they could do best. They were sensitive. They listened, and they cared about people.

You can perform similar ministries where you are. Take advantage of small opportunities and you will see changes begin in people's lives. Sooner or later God will give increase to the seeds of caring which you scatter.

Loneliness, alienation, uncertainty, and fatalism were all oppressively present in this desert city which masqueraded as a mecca of entertainment and happiness. For a while I thought that they were peculiarities of the place that became my "home" for six months.

But as I moved to a new location, and to more normal surroundings, I found that there are people everywhere who are bored, lonely, uncertain, and alienated.

The following four chapters suggest ways in which you can develop a productive, supporting personal ministry.

You *can* do it!

8. Two Ears, One Mouth

A Ministry of Listening

God may have given us two ears and only one mouth because he wants us to listen twice as much as we speak.

All around us there are despairing people, hurting for the lack of someone who will really listen to them. They have managed to cover years of seething discontent with a well-polished veneer—never daring to express their humanity for fear of the judgments of other people. No matter how serene and confident their outer appearance, they may now be enduring the most severe crisis of their lives.

Many of these complex experiences can be unraveled. Knotty frustrations can be untied. The burdensome guilt of sins can be lifted. Unfulfilled hopes can be released to become realities—if only someone will provide a starting point by sensitive listening.

Perhaps you can minister to some of these troubled

people by becoming a listening specialist. Consider the following essentials before you embark on such a delicate ministry:

1. *Listen confidentially.*

You are highly complimented when other people trust you enough to share their innermost humanity with you. If you accept this compliment, you must also be willing to accept the responsibility of a trust relationship. The confidences of that relationship must be well guarded at all times.

I recently heard of a clergyman who was responsible for devastating the lives of many people in his congregation. He was willing to accept their confidences but was not able to handle their trust responsibly. His public insinuations and "prayer requests" gave just enough information so that imaginations could run wild and arrive at distorted conclusions.

Can people trust you with their secrets, failures, doubts, frustrations and hopes? Can they have the confidence that you will respect their trust by not revealing their feelings and experiences to any other person—either directly or by shadowed innuendo?

If you have any doubt about your ability to listen confidentially, then this ministry is not for you at this time. But, if you honestly know that you *can* listen confidentially, then you can be an important expression of God's loving concern for individuals.

Listen unto others as you would have them listen unto you—confidentially.

2. *Listen without being judgmental.*

Many perplexed people need to talk to someone so that they can bring their clouded feelings into the light. This can help them view their experience more objectively.

They have heard many of the pious phrases which are frequently and easily offered as quick solutions. They probably *know* the difference between right and wrong.

But knowing is not always enough. There are times when powerful emotions are at odds with the intellect. So, it is not always helpful to tell someone that he or she is right or wrong. It is essential for that person to know that you are a special, nonjudging friend—concerned enough to invest the time to listen.

Judgmentalism undercuts the ministry of listening. As a listener you can never know all the factors which have brought the speaker to his or her present experience. Long years of severe pressures may have contributed to the complexities which are being shared. You may or may not understand. You might or might not agree. Your task is simply to listen.

Judgmental listeners tend to crush people. But it is never appropriate for any human being to crush another person intentionally. Neither is it appropriate for a listener to intrude into the private workings of the Holy Spirit in the life of another person—either judgmentally *or* lovingly. Just listen—and allow God to do his work, in his way, at his time—possibly through you.

A nonjudgmental listener is not concerned with placing blame. Hopefully he or she becomes a part of a healing process and recognizes that God is the ultimate healer.

Listen unto others as you would have them listen unto you—without being judgmental.

3. *Remain in control of yourself while you listen.*

People whose lives are being shaken need the stability of a listening friend who is not easily shocked. A listener who reveals a high degree of shockability will never know the privilege of helping people deal with their deepest needs.

Your attitude of acceptance of the speaker as a person, regardless of what he or she has said or done, can infuse him with hope. It can help him see that all is not lost—that there *is* a way to cope with his dilemma successfully.

Can you handle momentary rejection and hostility? There are extremely sensitive times when the person to whom you have been listening may seem to reject you. He may begin to fear that he has shown you too much of himself and become hostile toward you. Learn to expect this as a possible part of the healing process. It may reflect the approach or the aftermath of agonizing decision.

So, when rejection and hostility are present, don't lose your own balance. Resist the temptation to feel sorry for yourself. Don't lash out in your own defense. Remain available. Remember, in the beginning of this special relationship you accepted the compliment of trust and a responsibility of confidentiality. At this stage of the relationship your speaker is trusting you with another part of himself which is activated for its own reasons. The appearance of rejection and hostility may be a test of this relationship. It may be the final examination of the depth of the care that you profess to have for the person to whom you have been listening.

Can you remain in control of yourself in the event of apparent failure? If the person to whom you have been listening makes a poor decision or fails, will you reject him for his failure? Or, will you feel that you have failed to "set him straight"?

Remember, as a listener you are not a problem-solver. You are not responsible for the actions of another person. His struggles, failures, and victories are his own. You cannot make responsible decisions for another individual.

When a person fails, he needs a sensitive friend who will sympathize with the struggle which he endured before his failure. Your continuing acceptance and patience may provide the hope he needs in order to go on.

Listen unto others as you would have them listen unto you; remain in control of yourself.

4. *Listen for silence.*

Have you ever experienced absolute silence? I mean the complete lack of all sounds—no automobiles, no people, no airplanes overhead, no wind, not even the buzzing sounds of insects?

I had that rare privilege in the desert, miles from

the nearest town. I felt an eerie awesomeness. The simple thud of a dropping pebble, which would have gone unnoticed elsewhere, became startling. A whisper seemed irreverent.

For me, this was my most memorable worship experience. I stood there, alone, dwarfed by the surrounding mountains which seemed to have intruded their way into the desert by mistake, and found new meaning in the words, "Be still and know that I am God." I discovered, firsthand, the value of silence.

An effective listener grows to appreciate moments of silence. Too often we assume that nothing is being accomplished unless someone is talking. But, a good listener is willing to sit in silence and respect another person's need for creative thinking time. This is hard work.

Quiet spaces have special value as one individual shares his inner thoughts with another. These periods of silence allow time for collecting, organizing, and reorganizing thoughts. They are necessary moments of release from pressure. They provide opportunity to reveal thoughts that may be very difficult—when the speaker is ready.

When a person stops talking, don't assume that this is a signal for you to begin. By his pause he may be saying, "Let's both be quiet so that I can think about what I have just said or what I want to tell you next. In order to understand my words you must also understand my silences."

Allow the speaker to complete his own thoughts without interruption. If his thoughts seem unclear to you,

you may wish to say, "I don't think I understand what you mean—would you please repeat that?" But don't try to say it for him. When you ask questions, be sure that you don't pry. Allow the speaker to say what he wants to say. Don't force him to say more than he wants to reveal.

So, welcome the periods of silence. Don't let them frighten you into disrupting a train of thought. The moments of quiet which you provide may be your most vital contribution to the ministry of listening.

Listen unto others as you would have them listen unto you; respect the moments of silence.

Effective listening requires time and concentrated effort. It is hard work. I remember a day when I carried a burden which could have been lightened by the opportunity to talk to a good listener. I went to the logical person for help—a pastor. Opening the door to his office, I said, "Pastor, may I have a few moments to discuss something with you?" His comment was, "I'm glad you said 'a few moments' because I am very busy and don't have much time to give you." I passed a few pleasantries and left, still carrying my burden.

Who can tell how many sins and tragedies could be avoided . . . how many frustrations could be overcome . . . how many dreams could become realities, if only someone would invest the time to really listen.

Listen unto others as you would have them listen unto you. Someday you too may need the ministry of a listening specialist.

9. Going Around in Circles

A Ministry of Friendship

Have you ever felt that the world would be a wonderful place if it weren't for people? Occasionally the daily wear and tear of contact with our fellow human beings tends to drive us into isolation. We all need periodic times to be alone so that we can recharge ourselves.

But there is something about human nature that will not allow us to remain individual islands for very long. We are social creatures and crave contact with other people.

Outside the family, most people move in three relationship circles.

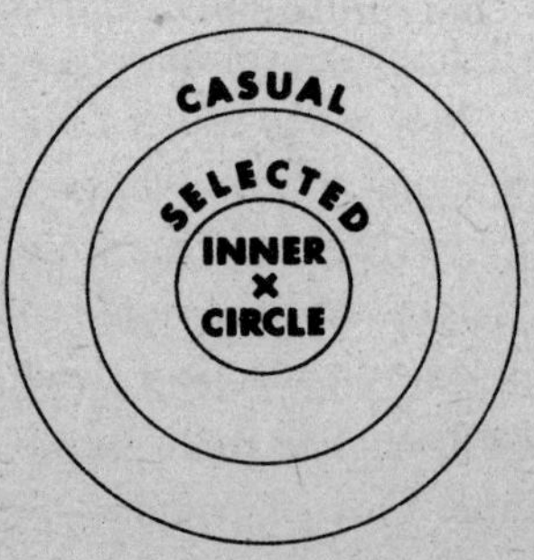

Imagine that you are standing at the center of the three circles.

The widest area around you includes acquaintances with whom you have casual contact. You talk with them at the bus stop, or you work with them each day. Some of them are your neighbors. They are people whom you meet at social or service club activities.

For the most part these widest relationships grow out of necessity, close geographical location, or coincidence of schedule.

The second, smaller circle contains selected social contacts. Most of these develop because of personal choice. You make a decision to include these people as your friends.

In this circle, choices are usually based on similar likes, dislikes, and lifestyles. The contacts are regular because of mutual enjoyment. You share invitations to each other's homes, with an element of reciprocity. (We had dinner at the Smiths' home last month. It's our turn to invite them this month.) Though you may enjoy associations in this group, there is still a thread of restraint involved. (You will invite the Smiths for a formal meal but probably would not call them at the last minute to ask them to join you for pizza in the kitchen.)

The smallest circle provides an opportunity for intimacy and support not possible in the larger circles. While the quantity of friends in this circle is usually small, the quality of comfortable acceptance and freedom is priceless. Jesus had this special kind of relationship with an inner core of people—Peter, James, and John.

An inner-circle friend is a person with whom you dare to be yourself. He allows you to be just what you are—without pretense. He does not try to manipulate you into being something different. With him, you don't have to be on your guard. You may say what you think, as long as it is you.

He understands your longings and actions which others misjudge. With him you breathe freely. He accepts your humanity, your little vanities, hates, and vicious sparks because he has them too. In sharing your imperfections with him, they become lost in the flow of his loyalty. You don't have to be careful.

Best of all, you can be still with an inner-circle friend. You don't have to prove anything.

You can cry with him, laugh with him, pray with him. Through it all he sees you, knows you, understands you, accepts you, and loves you.

I have a few friends like that, and I am grateful. I hope that I am learning to be that kind of friend to others.

It is only when severe difficulty arrives that the inner circle becomes clearly defined. Personal hard times put friendship to the test. Some friends may turn against you. Other friend-relationships will surprisingly evaporate like the morning mist. Some friendships will be temporarily suspended until fair weather returns. (These, however, will never be quite the same.)

When real difficulty comes, only a few people will tighten their ring of understanding and support around you. That inner circle, which seems indefinable when things are going well, suddenly becomes clear. Sometimes there may be only one other person there. But often, that is enough to help relieve pressures that would otherwise be unbearable.

We learn some valuable lessons from the Book of Job. It records a friendship ministry which started out well but ended in disaster.

When Job's three friends heard about his terrible calamity they traveled many miles to comfort him. They probably didn't know what to say or do, but they decided that it was important to be with their friend in his time of trouble.

They joined him in sympathetic weeping. They didn't say, "Now, Job, stop crying. You know that everything will turn out all right." Job had good reason to be grief-stricken. And his friends allowed him that privilege. They shared his grief, and in so doing helped to lighten his burden. They showed unusual sensitivity to his need for privacy by remaining silent for seven days and seven nights.

Unfortunately, they could not control their urge to talk after those days and nights of silence.

As soon as they opened their mouths their ministry deteriorated and they failed some of the basic tests of true friendship.

One by one they tried to fix the blame for what had happened on Job. This they had no right to do. His tragedy resulted from a contest between God and Satan. Job didn't know this—and certainly this friends didn't know it either. He didn't need to be kicked while he was down. Job needed friends who would help him rebuild his life regardless of the cause for its collapse.

To compound their mistake they tried to make God

responsible for their false accusations by saying, "The Lord told us these things." The Lord gets a lot of things blamed on him that are not his fault. And so it was with Job's friends. Later, God reprimanded them for misrepresenting him, and they were required to offer sacrifices for their own forgiveness.

There are people in all of your circles of acquaintances who need a friend to stand beside them.

These needs are ever-present opportunities. You cannot meet them all. The ministry of friendship cannot be forced or imposed on someone who is not receptive. It must develop naturally from a common bond that goes beyond the presence of a need.

The writer of Proverbs revealed the primary test of friendship when he said, "A friend loveth at all times." The thread that holds true friendship together is *constancy*.

Effective friends are constant in their availability. They are "on duty" when they are needed, but they can also keep a low profile without feeling hurt when not needed.

An acquaintance told me of a critical time in his life when he seriously considered committing suicide. After a sleepless night, he found himself standing by the open window of his ninth-floor city hotel room, ready to jump. As a last attempt to cling to life, he reached for the telephone and dialed a close friend, even though it was only 5:00 A.M. The friend listened to his desperation, helped him regain some perspective, and saved his life. The desperate man, now calmed, apologized for calling so early in the morning. His friend said, "Call me anytime you need me. I'm always available to you." Who can doubt the value of the reassuring availability of true friendship?

Real friendship remains constant when people are separated by time and distance. I have close friends who live many miles away. We may not see each other or communicate for months at a time. But when we do make contact we are able to pick up where we left off without having to rebuild the relationship. If I find a serious need in my life, they are the first people I call. Their friendship is more cherished than the contacts I have with many people who live nearby.

True friendship remains constant without being paid back. It is not based on repayment, nor is it destroyed by nonrepayment. It does not contain the "I-have-done-this-for-you,-therefore-you-owe-me-a-favor-of-equal-value" syndrome.

The ministry of friendship remains constant in times of difficulty. In fact, there is nothing like adversity to help one distinguish real friends from "fair weather" acquaintances. The advent of trouble usually shrinks the circle of friendship quite effectively.

If someone you know is experiencing hard times—a business failure, a marriage breakup, or other problem—you can be sure that some of their long-term, trusted acquaintances have deserted them. Maybe you can provide them with some stability through your friendly availability.

Real friendship remains constant through changing behavior patterns. In a possessive, manipulative relationship one person may say to another, "I will be your friend as long as I approve of your behavior. When I disagree with what you do, then I cannot be your friend." But a true friend recognizes that people are human; they make mistakes; they change; they sin. Taking this into account, a good friend remains constant and nonembarrassed when these forms of human nature show themselves in the life of another person.

You probably do not approve of the life style of Dawn, the prostitute in apartment number 2. I'm sure that Cathy and Scott did not approve either. But somehow they had learned to separate what she was as a person from what she did to earn a living—and they were able to extend the ministry of friendship.

Can you do the same?

Each circle of acquaintances provides you with multiple opportunities for a friendship ministry.

If your friendship is readily available,
If it can stretch across time and miles,
If it doesn't depend on being repaid,
If it can last through hard times,
If it can endure changing behavior patterns,
then it meets the test of constancy.

This is the kind of friendship that expresses growth in Christian love and understanding.

Looking for a ministry that an ordinary person can perform? Why not try the ministry of friendship?

You can be a friend now, right where you are.

10. Saying "Thank You" Convincingly

A Ministry of Appreciation

For the past fifteen years I have been involved in work directly related to the church. These ministries have required thousands of miles of travel, many hours of preparation, hundreds of speaking and teaching assignments, usually at no cost to the group benefiting from the service.

During that time a small group of people have invested extra time to share their thanks in a convincing way. These people stand out as rare gems of encouragement.

Few words are more satisfying to hear than "thank you," said convincingly. These are priceless grace notes which enhance the quality of life for each of us. Since a convincing "thank you" does not require extraordinary effort or unusual talent, the rarity of such expressions is surprising.

Phrases which are frequently repeated lose their convincing power. Familiarity dulls their message. The mere repetition of the words *thank you* may not be a sufficiently personal demonstration of your real feeling of gratitude.

You will be able to convey your sincere appreciation in a special way if you will add the dimension of creativity to your thank you.

Such creative expressions often fill individuals with powerful personal motivation to do their best. They can also help people to overcome handicaps and hardships which would otherwise seem insurmountable.

Several years ago I conducted four leadership training sessions for a small church. I had not asked for any pay, nor did I expect any. However, when the sessions were completed, I was presented with a creative expression of thanks. The people of that church gave me a leather-bound copy of a Bible version which I had wanted for a long time. I probably would not have bought such an expensive edition for myself, but I now use it every day. When I open its pages I think of the individuals in the church. They made their appreciation convincing by their creativity.

On another occasion I was paid well for speaking at a banquet. At the conclusion of the program the chairman said, "We know that coming here tonight required an evening away from your family. We would like you to take the floral arrangement on the head table to your wife as an additional indication of our thanks." Within two days I also received a handwritten note thanking me for my ministry. Their thank you was convincing because it was creative. It was different.

They had gone the second mile. And that second mile cost them only a postage stamp and a few extra moments of time.

Brief, handwritten notes are valuable tools for sharing your appreciation. Though they are simple, they can be worded creatively.

There are many people in church work who need to be thanked for their faithful, personal ministries. Organists, choir directors, soloists, custodians, secretaries, and teachers are often taken for granted. They should be told that their contributions are valuable.

Once, while visiting in the home of a church organist, I asked if she received any pay for her job. Opening the piano bench, she handed me a four-year accumulation of creative thank-you notes from her thoughtful pastor. "This is my pay," she said.

The fact that she had kept those notes for such a long time convinced me of their value.

Creative thank-you expressions need not be financially expensive. Many people have become accustomed to saying thank you with money. But, because of our affluence, money may be the least costly and least convincing item that we can give. Cash or a check, given without some written words of appreciation, can be cold and impersonal.

The time and thought which you apply to creating an expression of thanks are far more convincing than the financial value of a card or gift. When you invest extra time and effort in a creative thank you, the recipient knows that you cared enough to give something of yourself.

I know people who, with a few pieces of construction paper and some pictures clipped from a magazine, are able to take something of little financial value and create an item of priceless remembrance. Simple, inexpensive—but very convincing.

In addition to giving thanks, can you also be a gracious receiver of appreciation? Many people find it difficult to accept the thanks of others. But, the ministry or service which you have provided, though small to you, may have been exactly what the receiver needed to meet a large need in his life. Don't rob him of the opportunity to say thank you. Accept his thanks graciously and be glad that you were able to help.

Phillips Brooks, the famous preacher of the late 1800s, was disturbed that some members of his congregation had allowed walls of unforgiveness and ingratitude to grow between them. The walls had not sprung up intentionally, but developed out of personal reserve and thoughtlessness.

And so he preached a sermon on the theme, *The Time Is Short.* He spoke of the need to express words of forgiveness, appreciation, and encouragement to others. At the conclusion he said, "You who are letting your friend's heart ache for a word of appreciation or sympathy, which you mean to give him someday; if only you could know and see and feel, all of a sudden, that 'the time is short,' how it would break the spell! How you would go instantly and do the thing which you might never have another chance to do." *

---

* Lillian Eichler Watson, *Light from Many Lamps* (New York: Simon and Schuster, 1951).

His message was so persuasive that people who hadn't spoken to each other for years shook hands and embraced after the service. Others shared words of gratitude and encouragement which they had held inside for so long.

It was the beginning of a new spirit of unity in the congregation.

I visit a particular store owner several times each year as a part of my sales work. I always look forward to calling on her because she gives me a cordial welcome and treats me with respect. I have never known her to be disagreeable or out of sorts.

After one visit I commented to my wife, "You know, I really like that lady. She is one of the nicest people that I meet in business." Jean said, "Have you ever told her that?" I was stunned that I hadn't thought of it! Then I remembered Phillips Brooks's sermon. I determined that I would tell this lady how much I appreciate her.

On my next visit, as I prepared to leave her store, I said, "I always look forward to coming to your store because you treat me so kindly."

Well, you would have thought that I had handed her a thousand dollars. She broke into a broad smile, shot her hand across the counter to shake mine, and said, "Thank you. Thank you, thank you. You have just made my day."

I've come to believe that "making somebody's day" with a few words of honest appreciation is a valuable ministry.

Think of the people who touch your life each day—

teachers, pastors, friends, those who perform services for you. You appreciate them. Then why not tell them so? When a lesson, sermon, musical number or other service is especially helpful to you, express your creative thanks to the people who provided that help for you. You may be giving them the impetus to strengthen their own lives.

Set a goal for yourself. Plan to show creative appreciation to at least one person each day.

Show your thanks unto others as you would have them show their thanks to you; be convincing by being creative.

11. Everybody Needs a Barnabas

A Ministry of Encouragement

Liberace, Wayne Newton, Sammy Davis, Jr., and Sergio Franchi all had simultaneous engagements at hotels on the Las Vegas Strip. People jammed each of the plush entertainment rooms twice nightly to enjoy these talented headliners.

The fact that their work is supported by hundreds of ordinary individuals became evident when more than 23,000 workers in the culinary, stagehands' and musicians' unions went on strike. Within hours the showroom curtains descended, the bright lights went out, tourists evacuated the city, and the stars withdrew to their suites to await the outcome of the negotiations.

After several weeks the workers had made their point. Their important, supportive role was essential and could not be taken for granted.

In a similar way, the supportive ministries of ordinary people are essential to continued growth in the Body of Christ.

Saul, later known as Paul, and John Mark were well known in the early church. But they might not have achieved their positions of leadership if it hadn't been for the unique ministry of a lesser known personality, Barnabas. Almost every time Barnabas is mentioned in the Bible he is encouraging someone. This seems to have been his principle contribution to the growth of the church.

After Saul's conversion, Christians were afraid to accept him because of his previous anti-Christian activities. It was Barnabas who had the courage to step out from the group and take the risk to stand beside Paul and encourage him. As a result, this young convert was eventually accepted by the Christian community and went on to become a great missionary. He wrote more than one-third of the New Testament.

What might have happened to Paul if Barnabas had not been there to exercise the ministry of encouragement?

Similarly, John Mark needed an encourager. He had been a failure. He started out on a missionary journey and, for some unknown reason, turned back. His failure was so miserable that Paul refused to give him a second chance. He would not allow Mark to accompany him on a second trip.

But Barnabas, the encourager, stepped in once again. He took John Mark to his own home town and spent the necessary time to help him reestablish his life.

And it worked. Years later, while Paul was in prison,

he wrote to Timothy and requested that he bring Mark because he was profitable for the ministry.

Who knows what might have happened to John Mark if it hadn't been for Barnabas—an ordinary Christian who faithfully did what he could do best, encourage people.

Every person needs a Barnabas—someone who will encourage him or her to achieve his or her full potential. You can fulfill a vital ministry by being an encourager to others around you.

People will respond to your ministry of encouragement because it shows that you *believe in them.* Barnabas obviously believed in the potential of both Saul and Mark.

The completion of this book is a good example of the power of belief. Jean has been my best friend and encourager. She is also my wife. Without her the writing would probably not have been finished. Since she is a good cook, she understands that it is important to allow some things to simmer on the back burner to enhance the flavor of the final dish. So, she accepted the long spells when nothing was put down on paper. But when the typewriter began to click again, I would catch a glimpse of her sly smile saying, "I knew it would happen."

She never nagged, questioned, or cajoled. Nor did she doubt. She always spoke of "when" the writing would be finished, never "if." She believed in this project. But even more important, she believes in me. And that encourages me to achieve my potential.

Bill Pass, a close friend, is a respected vice-president

of his company. His wife, Sue, quietly says that she knew that he would be a vice-president long before it became a reality. Some women seem to have a sixth sense about their men. She didn't push or pressure him—but she knew. I'm sure that the combination of his competence and her supportive, encouraging confidence has made him successful.

Many people, especially those who have gone through difficult experiences, suffer from a poor self-image. They don't believe in themselves. Plagued by self-doubt, they fall far short of achieving their potential.

For some people the problem of self-doubt is so deep-seated that they require professional help. But for many, your encouragement can help banish the shadows of a poor self-image and restore a healthy belief in their own potential.

People also respond to encouragement because it *gives them hope.*

If Saul and Mark had been left to stand alone, they might have given up in despair. But, the presence of one other human being, Barnabas the encourager, gave them the sense that all was not lost. It gave them hope.

I once knew a lady whose husband became mentally ill. While confined to a hospital he attempted suicide several times. A psychiatrist encouraged the wife to visit briefly each day even though the visits were painful. As she left at the close of each visit she was advised to tell her husband that she would return the next day and that she expected to see him there—a promise, hope for just one more day.

The gentleman gradually became well and functions normally today. This small bit of encouraging hope may well have contributed to his recovery.

Dr. William A. Nolen pointed out the motivating power of hope in his book, *The Making of a Surgeon.** Referring to Jim Adams, a patient burned on over 80 percent of his body, Dr. Nolen said, "A logical question, of course, is, if the patient is suffering, if his condition is hopeless, if he was a burden to his family, and if they were in constant anguish from watching him suffer, then why did I, or any doctor, persist in our efforts to keep him alive? The answer lies in the word 'hopeless.' I don't know the origin of the adage 'Where there's life there's hope,' but, I can testify that whoever coined it sensed something deep within the soul of man. I might know by all the norms and standards of scientific medicine that Jim Adams would be dead within a week; still I didn't *know* it. The odds might be 2 million or 5 million to one that he would soon be dead, but as long as there was one chance, no matter how remote, that he might live, did I have the right to deny life to him? I'll answer the question: No. . . .

"Miracles—I use the term to signify phenomena that we simply can't explain—do occur. There is hardly a surgeon of any experience who hasn't on at least one occasion given a patient up for dead only to find that the patient makes a complete recovery—one that is unexplainable, in terms of scientific knowledge."

No situation, no person, is beyond hope. Never un-

---

* New York: Random House, 1970.

derestimate its power. As long as there is God, there is hope.

Your ministry of encouragement may be the spark that will help make life new again for someone.

Everybody needs a Barnabas—an ordinary person who is willing to be an encourager.

You can do it!

12. An Unfinished Symphony

Maintaining a Balanced Ministry

Franz Schubert's *Unfinished Symphony* is an orchestral classic. Part of its attraction lies in the fact that, as the title implies, it *is* unfinished.

Likewise, part of the attraction of reaching out to others is that there is always unfinished business. There is never a time when all of the needs have been met—never a season when all the ministries have been performed.

People you already know are growing and developing new needs, just as you and I do. New acquaintances, all with their own needs, are constantly moving into your circles of friendship. The opportunities, like the mercies of God, are new every morning. Indeed, sometimes the needs will appear to be frustratingly overwhelming.

In giving an ordination charge to a young ministerial candidate, a seasoned pastor said, "There will be many demands on your time. At first they will all seem like legitimate needs and you will want to respond to every one. But you will soon learn to set your priorities and stick to them. There will be times when you will have to say no if you wish to maintain your effectiveness."

None of us can meet all of the identifiable needs around us. I don't believe God expects us to.

How, then, are we to maintain a balanced base from which to minister effectively in the midst of so many opportunities?

First, as the preacher said to the young minister, we must set our own priorities and stick to them.

Parents who become embroiled in many outside activities at a time when a growing family needs care and attention may be sacrificing their most important ministry. The other needs which they are meeting in their outside associations are probably worthy causes. But, at least during the important period of family growth, activities which take them away from that vital task should be kept at a minimum.

Priorities change as life goes on. Responsibilities fall in different directions. Each new phase brings priorities and opportunities to stretch our ministries into different areas.

The periodic evaluation of activities in the light of our priorities will help us maintain balance in the midst of so many needs.

Accepting our own limitations can also provide a stabilizing influence for our ministries.

I do not have the capacity or ability to meet certain needs now. But I know that there are other people who do have the experience and equipment to meet them.

There is an individual who used to frustrate me to the point of anger. Each new contact seemed to be more destructive than the last. In my opinion, this person made unrealistic demands on me that I could not possibly meet.

At first, these episodes threw me off balance for days at a time. The needs which I couldn't meet, and the frustration of someone exerting unreasonable pressure on me, sent me into an emotional tailspin.

Over a period of many months I have come to accept my limitations in dealing with this person. Now, when a demand is made which I cannot meet, I simply say, "I can't help you with that now." If there is a request that I can handle, I do so.

For me, recognizing and accepting my own limitations has removed the emotional fallout from the frustration of this relationship.

As I came to know Cathy and Scott better, I realized that most of their personal ministries were spontaneous. For the most part, they did not have a deliberate, planned program for reaching out. Their personal outreach grew out of a ministering attitude. They really cared about people. And so, their ministries were a natural, normal outflow of their inner concern.

Remember the traveler who was robbed, beaten and left for dead? One man, out of three who passed by, stopped to help him. Why was it the Samaritan who took practical pity on the unfortunate traveler, and not the priest or Levite? Was it because he had an organized program for helping people? Probably not. His help grew out of a caring attitude which led him to minister to others whenever and wherever the needs arose.

And so it was with Cathy and Scott. Their ministering seemed to be as natural as breathing, and it brought some encouraging responses.

Through their close contact with Martha, the Italian seamstress, they were able to have serious discussions with her about the spiritual dimensions of her life. They also helped her find some assistance for her emotionally disturbed son.

Though Dawn continued to ply her trade, she began to meet with a Sunday afternoon Bible study group and showed an awakening interest in God. (Fortunately, Scott and Cathy were able to recommend a group where they knew that Dawn would be treated as a person, in spite of her profession. Would a known prostitute be welcome in your church or study group?)

Tania, closer to stardom than ever, "adopted" Scott and Cathy as her unofficial, personal confidants. She shared her hopes and fears with them. They saw her as she really was—a privilege which she gave to very few people.

There were other encouraging responses. But, the symphony goes on. New chords, some minor, some major, are being added each day. It never ends.

What about Kate, in number 12? Fortyish, attractive, intelligent but, by her own admission, a loser. Whether her losing is the result of a continuing conspiracy of circumstances or the result of her own attitudes is hard to determine. Two marriages, one to an alcoholic, the other to a gambler, ended in disaster. She lost her $100-per-week job. Other employment in her area is based on "who you know," not on what you can do. Her rent is due in five days. It will take six weeks to process her unemployment claim and several weeks longer to receive her check. She has no friends or relatives who are willing to take another chance on a "loser." Underneath her blasé façade she is scared, and thinking of suicide (only to fear that she may fail at that also).

Who will help Kate? Cathy and Scott can't do it all.

The presence of police at the door of apartment 20 indicated that twenty-three-year-old Nancy had gone one step further than Kate. She had *tried* suicide as an escape from the beatings inflicted by her common-law husband. She has no money, no friends.

Who will minister to Nancy? How?

And what of crippled, seventy-six-year-old Mrs. Baily, "living" alone behind closed drapes in number 3. Once each week she manages, with the help of a walker, to shuffle a few steps to her open mailbox, usually to find it empty again. Her only contact with the outside world is the person who delivers her Meals-on-Wheels lunch each day promptly at 11:55 A.M.

Who will minister to Mrs. Baily?

So, you see, the symphony *is* unfinished. The needs I have described are probably different from those that are present in your circle of acquaintances. But the types of needs don't really matter. The fact remains that, wherever you are, the needs are there as opportunities for your personal ministry.

Who will meet needs like these? Spectacular people with special talents and abilities? A few, maybe . . .

But, for the most part, if they are to be met at all, it will be by ordinary Christians like you—people who faithfully do what they can do best.

13. Epilog: Ordinary, Special People

Ministering Expressions of God's Care

During the seven months between Memorial Day and Christmas, we transformed "The Gallagher house" into our own place.

As a part of the Advent celebration we invited twenty-five people to share an evening of music in our new home. The pine scent of freshly cut evergreen boughs spread an old fashioned Christmas aroma through the house. The faces of our friends seemed especially warm and happy as they reflected the highlights of the candles placed strategically in the living room.

John and Susan were there. Their ministry of hospitality was our first experience of "beginning to belong" in a new community where we knew no one. And, because John is a skilled counselor, he had been a gentle, understanding listener on several critical occasions.

As I looked at George and Frances, associates in a

real estate business, I recalled a day when we had become quite discouraged, thinking that we would never find a house that we could afford. Frances's ministry of positive encouragement kept us going. And, sure enough, with her sensitive skill she finally matched our needs with the house for us—the time was right.

Jill and Geri have an unusual alertness to needs that require practical attention. I thought back to one of the many days when we were packing for the move from our temporary apartment to the new house. Since we did all of the moving ourselves after regular working hours, it was a sizable and tiring job. We were exhausted. And somehow, there were always more boxes to carry down from the second-floor apartment.

Jill and Geri caught sight of the needs. They seemed to materialize from nowhere. Without saying anything about it, they moved right in and began to carry boxes and bureau drawers. Nobody asked them to help—they just did it. We will always be grateful for their sensitive, practical ministry.

Soon after moving to town we discovered Don, Shirley, Barry, and Edith. They are fun to be with. The moments we spend with them have helped to make some heavy times lighter. Their ministry to us is friendly mirth.

And then there was Pearl, in her brilliant, Christmasy red dress. From the first day we moved in, her scintillating personality has made us feel as if we always belonged next door to her. Hers is a ministry of welcome and brightness. She lights up our lives.

John, our architect friend, exercised a money-saving

ministry for us. By willingly sharing his expert advice, he helped us reduce the cost of heating system repairs by $250.00.

One by one, as I looked at each person, I realized that everyone in the room had contributed an important ministry to us.

They are not spectacular people, with extraordinary talents. But they are special to us because they minister out of what they are.

I do not fully understand why it seems so easy for us to dwell on our liabilities . . . to underestimate our potential . . . to think that we have little to offer.

Perhaps it is because we are so familiar with ourselves that we do not recognize the freshness and value of our assets as they relate to other people's needs.

I believe that God has equipped each of us with capacities to minister to other people out of what we are. These capacities are shaped, stretched, developed and refined by our experiences.

Our personal ministries cannot be programmed. They shrivel and die when we try to force them into some artificial, step-by-step procedure. Attempts to confine them to contrived situations stifle their spontaneity and their spirit.

They flow out of the lives of people who have learned to accept others where they are

—people who respect the individuality, personhood, worth and potential of one another;

—people for whom relationships are opportunities for appreciation, not manipulation;

—people who minister, not out of guilt or responsibility, but out of the vitality of who they are becoming.

As you and I grow in our openness to God and people, we become the ministering expressions of his care to those around us.